# WOMEN WHO WIN

Laila Ali

Cynthia Cooper

Lindsay Davenport

Mia Hamm

Martina Hingis

Chamique Holdsclaw

Marion Jones

Anna Kournikova

Michelle Kwan

Lisa Leslie

Gabrielle Reece

Dorothy "Dot" Richardson

Sheryl Swoopes

Venus & Serena Williams

CHELSEA HOUSE PUBLISHERS

WOMEN WHO WIN

# Laila Ali

*Cindy Dyson*

*Introduction by*
HANNAH STORM

CHELSEA HOUSE PUBLISHERS
*Philadelphia*

JB.
Ali
Dyson

*Frontis:* Training is a vital part of any successful boxer's career. Laila knew that she would have to rely on more than her famous Ali name when she climbed into the ring. Here she wraps her hands in preparation for a fight.

CHELSEA HOUSE PUBLISHERS

Editor in Chief: Sally Cheney
Director of Production: Kim Shinners
Production Manager: Pamela Loos
Art Director: Sara Davis
Production Editor: Diann Grasse

Staff for Laila Ali
Editor: Sally Cheney
Associate Editor: Benjamin Kim
Associate Art Director: Takeshi Takahashi
Layout by D&G Limited.

The Chelsea House World Wide Web address is
http://www.chelseahouse.com

First Printing

1 3 5 7 9 8 6 4 2

Library of Congress Cataloging-in-Publication Data

Dyson, Cindy.
  Laila Ali / Cindy Dyson.
    p. cm.— (Women who win)
Includes bibliographical references (p. ) and index.
  ISBN 0-7910-6537-5 (alk. paper)
  1. Ali, Laila—Juvenile literature. 2. Boxers (Sports)—United States—
Biography—Juvenile literature. 3. Women boxers—United States—
Biography—Juvenile literature. [1. Ali, Laila. 2. Boxers (Sports) 3.
Women—Biography. 4. African Americans—Biography.] I. Title. II. Series.


GV1132.A42D97 2001
796.83'092—dc21
[B]                                                      2001028906

3065200112 9370

# CONTENTS

# WOMEN WHO WIN

## Hannah Storm
### *NBC Studio Host*

You go girl! Women's sports are the hottest thing going right now, with the 1900s ending in a big way. When the U.S. team won the 1999 Women's World Cup, it captured the imagination of all sports fans and served as a great inspiration for young girls everywhere to follow their dreams.

That was just the exclamation point on an explosive decade for women's sports—capped off by the Olympic gold medals for the U.S. women in hockey, softball, and basketball. All the excitement created by the U.S. national basketball team helped to launch the Women's National Basketball Association (WNBA), which began play in 1997. The fans embraced the concept, and for the first time, a successful and stable women's professional basketball league was formed.

I was the first ever play-by-play announcer for the WNBA—a big personal challenge. Broadcasting, just like sports, had some areas with limited opportunities for women. There have traditionally not been many play-by-play opportunities for women in sports television, so I had no experience. To tell you the truth, the challenge I faced was a little scary! Sometimes we are all afraid that we might not be up to a certain task. It is not easy to take risks, but unless we push ourselves we will stagnate and not grow.

Here's what happened to me. I had always wanted to do play-by-play earlier in my career, but I had never gotten the opportunity. Not that I was unhappy—I had been given studio hosting assignments that were unprecedented for a woman and my reputation was well established in the business. I was comfortable in my role . . . plus I had just had my first baby. The last thing I needed to do was suddenly tackle a new skill on national television and risk being criticized (not to mention, very stressed out!). Although I had always wanted to do play-by-play, I turned down the assignment twice, before reluctantly agreeing to give it a try. During my hosting stint of the NBA finals that year, I traveled back and forth to WNBA preseason games to practice play-by-play. I was on 11 flights in 14 days to seven different cities! My head was spinning and it was no surprise that I got sick. On the day of the first broadcast, I had to have shots just so I could go on the air without throwing up. I felt terrible and nervous, but I survived my first game. I wasn't very good but gradually, week by week,

I got better. By the end of the season, the TV reviews of my work were much better—*USA Today* called me "most improved."

During that 1997 season, I witnessed a lot of exciting basketball moments, from the first historic game to the first championship, won by the Houston Comets. The challenge of doing play-by-play was really exciting and I loved interviewing the women athletes and seeing the fans' enthusiasm. Over one million fans came to the games; my favorite sight was seeing young boys wearing the jerseys of female players—pretty cool. And to think I almost missed out on all of that. It reinforced the importance of taking chances and not being afraid of challenges or criticism. When we have an opportunity to follow our dreams, we need to go for it!

Thankfully, there are now more opportunities than ever for women in sports (and other areas, like broadcasting). We thank women, like those in this series, who have persevered despite lack of opportunities—women who have refused to see their limitations. Remember, women's sports has been around a long time. Way back in 396 B.C. Kyniska, a Spartan princess, won an Olympic chariot race. Of course, women weren't allowed to compete, so she was not allowed to collect her prize in person. At the 1996 Olympic games in Atlanta, Georgia, over 35,600 women competed, almost a third more than in the previous Summer Games. More than 20 new women's events have been added for the Sydney, Australia, Olympics in 2000. Women's collegiate sports continues to grow,spurred by the 1972 landmark legislation Title IX, which states that "no person in the United States shall, on the basis of sex, be excluded from participation in, be denied the benefits of, or be subjected to discrimination under any educational program or activity receiving federal financial assistance." This has set the stage for many more scholarships and opportunities for women, and now we have professional leagues as well. No longer do the most talented basketball players in the country have to go to Europe or Asia to earn a living.

The women in this series did not have as many opportunities as you have today. But they were persistent through all obstacles, both on the court and off. I can tell you that Cynthia Cooper is the strongest woman I know. What is it that makes Cynthia and the rest of the women included in this series so special? They are not afraid to share their struggles and their stories with us. Their willingness to show us their emotions, open their hearts, bare their souls, and let us into their lives is what, in my mind, separates them from their male counterparts. So accept this gift of their remarkable stories and be inspired. Because you, too, have what it takes to follow your dreams.

# 1

## INTO THE RING

It was a Friday night, October 8, 1999, at the Turning Stone Casino in Verona, New York. The casino ballroom was sold out, filled to capacity with 2,800 boxing fans. Most of them had come to see the debut fight of one woman—Laila Ali.

The match, situated among casino slot machines and game tables, looked like most fights—sleaze and glamour side by side. The scene had all the ingredients of a major bout: the cigar-wielding promoter in the corner, the loud boxing commissioner, the muscled fighters, the pressing reporters, the eager fans, and the light-bathed ring.

Laila shrugged off her long, white, hooded robe and ducked under the ropes. Facing her was April Fowler, a 27-year-old waitress from Michigan City, Indiana. April had fought only once before. She'd been knocked out.

Laila weighed 166 pounds and stood 5-feet, 10-inches tall. She was lean and eager. Beside her April looked flabby and doomed. Laila shut out the cheering fans and her fears and focused on April and the fight ahead.

When the bell rang, April charged. She turned her head and clamped her eyes shut as her fists flailed at Laila.

In Laila's fourth match, she faced Crystal "Brave Heart" Arcand of Canada. Laila's punching power proved too much for the Canadian, scoring Ali another first-round victory by knockout.

Laila backed her off with straight jabs, then a furious combination. Laila moved in for a left-right combination to April's jaw, knocking her back. April thudded to the canvas 31 seconds into the fight.

"Get up! Get up!" Laila screamed, standing over April with her fists cocked. But April stayed down, and Laila won her first professional fight in the first round with a knockout. When a fighter is knocked to the mat and doesn't get up within eight seconds, her loss is labeled a knockout.

Laila glanced down at her father, sitting ringside. She leaned through the ring ropes and kissed him on the cheek.

"My father said he was proud of me," Laila said later. "From the look in his eyes, I could tell he was proud of me."

Shortly before the fight, Laila's father had entered the ballroom as the ring announcer introduced "a man who needs no introduction," Muhammad Ali. The crowd craned their necks to watch Muhammad take his seat by the ring. A chant rose up, "Ali! Ali! Ali!"

As soon as Laila's fight ended, fans rushed forward toward Muhammad, pressing for autographs and handshakes. The ring announcer had to beg them to clear the aisles.

Laila knew most of the fans had come because of her father. She knew that if it weren't for his name, she'd be just another fledgling fighter. She knew that the reporters—who had come from as far away as Germany, England, and Japan, had come to see if she would live up to the standard her father had set decades before.

After the fight, reporters surrounded Laila. They commented on how much Laila's fighting

style resembled her father's. Comparisons were inevitable, but Laila wanted to make sure people knew she intended to be a strong fighter in her own right.

"I wasn't trying to be like my father," Laila insisted. "I'm not my father. I'm me."

Laila's father, Muhammad, is the most well-known boxer in the world. He captured the world's attention in a way no other fighter ever has.

"He possessed all the attributes of a perfect hero: He was young, handsome, brash, witty, irreverent, chance-taking, religious, clean, and entertaining," wrote Ferdie Pacheco, Muhammad's fight doctor. "But, best of all, he was simply, far and away, the greatest fighter of his time."

Laila Ali's pro boxing debut lasted only 31 seconds as she knocked out Indiana waitress April Fowler in the first round. Here, Laila's powerful right connects with Fowler's jaw. Fowler fell and didn't get up, ending the fight.

The Ali family, including famous dad, Muhammad, come out to cheer Laila from ringside. Having her family's support is an important part of Laila's success.

Muhammad came to the world's attention in 1960 as Cassius Clay when he won the light-heavyweight division in the Olympic Games in Rome. Four years later, he announced he had converted to the Nation of Islam—a religion that had gained popularity with American blacks during the 1960s and 1970s. Cassius changed his name to Muhammad Ali. He would go on to become the heavyweight champion in 1964. He defended his title until 1967 when he refused to be drafted into the Vietnam War. He was stripped of his title, barred from boxing and sentenced to five years in jail. But Muhammad fought, filing an appeal and spending only one day in jail. By 1971, his appeal had reached the Supreme Court, which overturned his indictment unanimously.

In 1974, Muhammad reclaimed his title. In 1978 he fought challenger Leon Spinks and lost. But Muhammad fought Spinks again and regained the title of heavyweight champion of the world for an unprecedented third time in September 1978.

But it was more than his title that made Muhammad "The Greatest." His athleticism was legendary. He was a big man, but moved with the speed and precision of much lighter fighters. His calling-card slogan, "float like a butterfly, sting like a bee," described Muhammad's fighting style perfectly. He moved with grace and ease around the ring, seeming at times to play with his opponent. But his punches were devastating. He had successfully combined the lightweight fast footwork and easy dodges with the power of the heavyweight punch.

He was also handsome. Watching Muhammad move, in the ring or out, captivated people. His body was famous for its beauty and grace. When he spoke, people were drawn to his handsome face.

Muhammad was known as a talker. He developed an arrogant way of speaking to the press that made boxing fans either hate or love him. At times he was playful, tossing subtle jokes and rhyming poems into his interviews. At other times he was intimidating, raising his fist at a reporter or glaring into a camera—all playful gestures tinged with something threatening. Muhammad bragged about his skills, predicting knockouts against his opponents, calling them too ugly to fight him. But he always backed up his bravado.

As early as 1977, Muhammad's health began deteriorating. A physical had shown signs of kidney and neurological damage. In

1980, Muhammad tried another comeback, and lost to Larry Holmes. By then many observers saw that Muhammad had lost speed, and that something was wrong.

Muhammad would be diagnosed with punch-drunk syndrome, a deterioration of the mid-brain, caused by repeated shocks. Later he would be diagnosed with Parkinson's disease, possibly brought on by repeated blows to the head. Parkinson's has slowed Muhammad's speech and movements. He suffers with tremors and will likely progress with less and less control of his movements, speech, and comprehension.

Laila was born after her father's boxing career had fizzled out, but she heard the stories. She listened to tales of Muhammad's brilliant 1964 defeat of heavyweight champion Sonny Liston, of Muhammad's conversion to Islam and his controversial opposition to the Vietnam War, and of his legendary fights against Joe Frazier, Ken Norton, and George Foreman.

Other boxers have captured the limelight in recent years, but Muhammad holds a special place in sports history. When boxing fans speak of "the greatest" or the "champion," they are still referring to Muhammad Ali.

The night Laila entered the ring for the first time, she brought all that history with her. And she brought it to a sport that desperately needed it. Women's boxing is a new sport. It doesn't have a large following yet, and many people don't take female fighters seriously. But Laila set out to change that.

"She has restored a legendary name to boxing and infused it with a high-octane mix of youth, athleticism, beauty and ambition," wrote journalist John de St. Jorre. "Women's

boxing is in the process of moving from sideshow to serious sport. With Ali in the spotlight . . . women's boxing is nearing showtime."

In his prime, Muhammad Ali was the fastest, hardest-hitting boxer in the ring, known for his slogan "Float like a butterfly, sting like a bee."

## 2

# BORN INTO BOXING ROYALTY

Throughout his career, women flocked to Muhammad. He would eventually marry four times. His first marriage, before his conversion to Islam, was brief. Muhammad chose a Muslim woman, Belinda, for his second wife. They had four children together.

In 1974, Muhammad met a stunning woman named Veronica Porche. Veronica had just won a beauty contest that would make her the poster girl for a fight between Muhammad and George Foreman in Zaire, Africa. The fight, promoted as the "Rumble in the Jungle," drew lots of media attention.

Veronica's beauty and poise captivated Muhammad. He invited her to accompany his entourage to Zaire, where the two began an affair. Belinda closed her eyes to Mohammed's unfaithfulness for more than a year. But eventually, she demanded Muhammad choose between her and Veronica. Muhammad chose Veronica and divorced Belinda.

In 1977, Veronica and Muhammad married. They already had one child, Hana, who was almost a year old.

Although Laila was knocked down in the first round of her bout against Karen Bill, she got up and went on to win the fight in the third round by technical knockout. It was the first real challenge Laila had received to her talents in the ring.

Being the daughter of "The Greatest" wasn't always easy. But Laila has worked hard to step outside the shadow of her legendary father, three-time heavyweight champion Muhammad Ali. Here they are together after Laila's win against Kendra Lenhart.

Laila came along a year and a half later, on December 30, 1977. The new family lived in Marina Del Rey, California. They were famous, rich, and adored. Laila was just three years old when her father fought his last fight—a loss in 1981.

Laila was a quiet child, preferring to play with dolls by herself, while Hana roughhoused with Muhammad. Hana remembered Muhammad as a devoted father during the years he was around.

"I can remember waking up very early in the morning, running over to Laila's room to get her up," Hana wrote in her tribute book to her father, *More Than a Hero.* "Together we would run down the stairs into the kitchen, to make an 'interesting' cup of coffee for Dad." The girls would pour any liquids they could find into a cup.

"My father would always drink it all up, then kiss us and tell us how good it was.

"After that Laila would lie by the fireplace and draw as I sat on Daddy's lap pretending to write in cursive. . . . The greatest gift a parent can ever give to a child, my father gave to us time and time again—himself."

But Hana also remembered times when Muhammad was away training for fights. She and Laila had a governess who helped care for them, but they missed their father and hated those times when he was gone.

In 1986, when Laila was eight, Veronica and Muhammad divorced. Laila and her sister lived with their mother, seeing Muhammad only during vacations to his farm in Berrien Springs, Michigan, and on brief visits during the year. Muhammad had married a woman named Lonnie. He and his new wife then had another child. Laila never felt close to Muhammad. He was too unlike her and too distant.

But once a year he would fly to Los Angeles, gathering all of his (then) eight children and spend time with them as a family.

"I remember Laila, Dad, and I driving down Wilshire Boulevard . . . " Hana wrote. "We were in Dad's brown Rolls-Royce. The top down, as usual, and I can still feel the wind blowing my hair against my face. . . . Every summer, Dad would fly in the rest of our brothers and sisters—who weren't living with us, since they were all from other marriages. . . . Anyway, we'd often all pile into the car and go driving all around Los Angeles—with the top down. People on the road would see Dad and shout out: 'Hi, Champ!' 'You're the Greatest! or 'Oh, my God it's Muhammad Ali!' Those were the Glory Days."

After watching boxer Christy Martin on a televised bout, an 18-year-old Laila decided she would try her luck in the ring. It was the first time Laila realized that women boxed and it signaled a major turning point in her life.

Despite the yearly visits, Laila didn't know her father well. While Hana became daddy's girl, levelheaded and eager, Laila refused to get close to her father.

She also refused to participate in sports. She knew and respected her father's famed career and athleticism but didn't show any signs of being interested or talented as an athlete.

As a teen, Laila began to rebel. The family had moved to Malibu, where Laila grew up privileged. She felt drawn to people who weren't.

"Everyone else was trying to get out of the ghetto," she said. "I was trying to get in. I wanted to experience the other side."

She stole her mother's car more than once before she was legally old enough to drive. She also started shoplifting. When she was fifteen, she was caught shoplifting and put on probation. A year later, in 1995, she got caught shoplifting again. She had taken a tank top after an incident she described as resulting from "hanging out with the wrong crowd." She came before the same judge who had sentenced her before.

"He knew who my father was, knew my background. He was like, Why is this girl doing this?"

The judge ordered Laila to spend three months in a facility for juvenile delinquents.

"He didn't convict me—I don't have a record. But it was his way of making me snap out of what I was doing," Laila said.

Those months were a tough time for Laila. But she came out with better sense.

When released, Laila took manicuring classes. By age 18, Laila had a job at a beauty salon in Marina Del Rey and settled into her life. Soon she was running her own nail salon while taking business classes at Santa Monica City College.

One night, Laila switched on the television. Christy Martin, one of boxing's best female boxers, was fighting. Laila was mesmerized.

"It was the first time I knew women boxed," she said. "I thought, Oh my god! I can do that!"

The images of the fight stayed with Laila long after she turned off the television. She wondered if she could do it.

"There would be a lot of pressure on me because of who my father is," she thought. "Would I really like it? Do I want to live my life publicly? How hard would it be?"

# 3

# FOLLOWING HER HISTORY

L aila was thinking about entering a dangerous and controversial sport. A few boxers have died after taking
punches in the ring, and many have suffered injuries. In
some countries, boxing is banned, and there are some
boxing observers even in the United States who think the
sport should be outlawed.

For female boxers, the sport is even more difficult. Only
a few women make a living boxing, and most just barely.

Women's boxing itself isn't new, but it is new in terms of
being recognized as an official sport. Reports of women
fighting in the ring go back to the 1700s in England, where
fights between women were occasionally staged for the
entertainment of men. In these fights, women didn't box so
much as flail, scratch, kick, and maul each other.

In the 1800s, women in the United States began fighting in the ring at country fairs and exhibitions. Most of the
women who fought were the sisters and daughters of exhi-
bition fighters, who made their livings roaming from town
to town staging fights for entertainment. Women born into
these fighting families often fought in outfits designed

Traveling all the way to China, Laila showed her talents against SWAT team member
and former prison guard Kristina King. Laila's first televised fight ended in the fourth
round when she was declared the winner by technical knockout.

Boxer Christy Martin celebrates a victory over Deirdre Gogarty at the MGM Grand in Las Vegas, 1996.

more for show than for sport. One woman fought in a red velvet gown topped off with a pair of boxing boots and gloves.

Usually these fights were a novelty, luring audiences to the main fights between men. But some of the women who fought took it seriously, training and developing their skills.

In the 1970s, with the rise of the women's liberation movement, women made their first real forays into boxing as sport. But no official organizations tracked their ranks or staged professional quality matches.

In 1977 a woman became the first sanctioned judge at a heavyweight title fight. During the 1980s, as fighting sports like karate, judo, kickboxing, and boxerobics gained popularity, women joined in. Some found they liked the demanding exercises and the challenge of sparring or practicing real punches and kicks with real opponents.

Women liked fighting-style exercise because it not only gave them athletic bodies but also confidence to defend themselves. Soon women began entering amateur boxing programs like the Golden Gloves. In 1982, Jill Lafler filed and won a lawsuit to be admitted as a Golden Gloves contestant.

But most female fighters weren't taken seriously. Part of the problem was the "foxy boxing" shows put on at bars. Scantily clad and nude women clawed and whacked at each other for the entertainment of male audiences. When people thought of female fighters, these were the women they imagined—not the well-trained, fully-clothed boxers with genuine skills.

Meanwhile women began to be a presence at men's fights like never before. Through most of the century, fights were all about men. The combatants, the audience, the judges, the promoters, the referees, the doctors, and the trainers were all men. The only women at a fight were usually the infamous ring girls, who paraded around the ring in bathing suits and high heels holding cards that announced the number of the next round. But by the 1980s, more women could be seen watching fights.

By the 1990s, enough women had entered the sport to create a pool of talented fighters. At last, women had a shot at making a career out of the sport. In 1993, USA Boxing recognized women as boxers after losing a court case.

As women's boxing gained popularity, some people worried that women would be hurt. Male boxers were plagued by injuries like brain damage, facial scarring, and diseases such as Parkinson's that may be linked to head trauma. People worried that women would be even more vulnerable to these injuries. USA Boxing quickly adopted special rules and regulations to govern women's amateur boxing that would give women extra protection. Professional boxing associations soon followed with the same regulations.

Women's boxing rounds last two minutes, rather than the three-minute rounds that men fight. Women are also required to take a pregnancy test before a match and must wear chest protectors.

In the mid-1990s, a network of groups was developed to foster women in boxing as professionals. There are now governing bodies for women's boxing in amateur and professional tournaments. There are also trainers and promoters who take on women as serious fighters and television channels that broadcast female fights.

Today the boom in women's boxing has led to an estimated 2,000 women across the country registered as amateur boxers and more than 700 as professional boxers.

But female boxing still suffers from its history as a novelty or as a catfight. The pool of well-trained women boxers is small. And television coverage—which is the means by which fighters gain public attention and notoriety for themselves—is sparse.

At the same time, some boxing fans have observed that women's boxing is tougher and

Practicing on the speed bag sharpens a boxer's reflexes, quickness, and coordination—skills Laila uses to their utmost when she fights.

provides a better show than men's boxing. For example, in March 1996, Christy Martin and Deidre Gogarty were scheduled to fight as a warm-up to Mike Tyson and Frank Bruno's heavyweight contest. The fight was broadcast on pay-per-view television with 1.1 million viewers. Fans were impressed with Christy and Deidre's fight, which was much more exciting than the men's match. Many people say this fight alone deserves a lot of credit for popularizing women's boxing.

Women boxers often face different obstacles than men do. Women fighters are sometimes promoted more because of their appearances than their boxing skills. One commentator dismisses women's boxing as "'Baywatch' with gloves on." More than a few cheerleaders, topless dancers, and models have been promoted as boxers.

This was the status of the sport Laila considered entering. But one day she decided to give it a try. She went to the L.A. Boxing Gym in Los Angeles. No one knew who she was. She started a class, thinking more about getting in shape than beginning a professional career. Every night she went to the gym, gaining strength and speed.

"First, it was a form of exercise," she says. "But deep down inside, I was trying to see if I had the talent to be a professional boxer. You find out by working with a trainer and asking people who know. They told me 'Yeah.'"

Laila decided to go for it. Veteran trainer Kevin Morgan agreed to take her on.

Now Laila had to tell her father. Laila knew he wouldn't like it. In the past he had said that the idea of women boxing conflicted with his Muslim beliefs. Laila, however, was the only one of his children who didn't follow her father's religious beliefs.

"My father and I are very alike," Laila explained. "We both do what we want to do. Sometimes what I want to do isn't what my dad wants me to do, so we bump heads. Like, for example, my dad is Muslim and all my sisters were raised Muslims, but I'm the one who was like, 'I don't want to be a Muslim.' His life revolves around his religion, and that's part of the reason he doesn't feel women should fight. I respect that, but it's not going to stop me."

In January, Laila met with Muhammad, determined to convince him to support her.

"Daddy," she remembers saying, "I want to tell you I'm going into professional boxing. I love you, and I want your support, but whether you give it or not, I'm going to do this."

Muhammad tried to talk her out of it. "Have you been hit?" he asked. "Have you been knocked down?"

"I'm not going to get hurt," she answered. "I'm going to fight women, not men. And I have your genetics."

Muhammad knew he couldn't talk his daughter out of it. Instead, he rose from his chair and raised his fists to give her a quick sparring lesson. Laila threw some fast jabs, backing her father into a corner.

Muhammad gave up. "You're good," he said. "I don't have to give you any pointers."

"I was surprised by his quickness," Laila said. "He popped me, but I surprised him too."

That's all Laila needed. She knew her father wasn't thrilled with her choice, but he'd support her regardless.

"I think my dad is pleased I'm an independent thinker," she said, "but if he could program my brain not to be a fighter, he would."

"I don't think it is necessarily natural for me just because of my father. I really wasn't involved with his boxing career, [since] I was too young at the time. Boxing was kind of separate from me then. I'm sure there is something within me that I cannot explain that draws me to it."

Veronica, who wasn't thrilled about Laila's decision either, said that part of what drew Laila to boxing was the chance to get closer to her father.

"It's not a simple thing to answer what motivates her," she said, "but I suspect that this is a way for Laila to be closer to her father and to finally bond with him."

Laila agreed that boxing could be the beginning of a new relationship with Muhammad.

"He's naturally going to see himself in me," Laila said. "But for the first time, I think he actually can see that 'this is my child.'"

# 4

# EASY WINS

News that Laila planned to become a fighter caught the media's attention. Dozens of newspapers, magazines, and television shows produced stories about her decision to follow in Muhammad's footsteps.

Reporters repeatedly asked her if she was worried that taking punches would damage her brain as it had her father's.

Muhammad, then 56, shuffled when he walked and spoke in a whisper, all due to Parkinson's disease. Watching her father become less physically able was tough for Laila, but she tried to keep it in perspective. Again and again, Laila told reporters that she planned her career to avoid such damage.

"My father stayed in the ring a lot longer than I intend to," Laila said. "He fought for years, and his strategy was to let fighters beat on him to wear themselves out, so he took a lot more beating than I plan on taking. I'm going to make some money, win a world title and move on."

Laila's favorite of her father's fights is his famous 1974 bout with George Foreman in Zaire. Nicknamed the "rope-

Facing a powerful boxer like Laila Ali in the ring means risking a first-round knockout. Here Laila sends opponent Marjorie Jones to the canvas 68 seconds into their fight.

Retired cruiserweight fighter Johnny "Ya Ya" McClain met Laila at a party and was immediately attracted to her. He later became her assistant trainer and her manager. The two were married in August 2000.

a-dope," Muhammad took a beating during the fight, purposefully wearing his opponent out to make a comeback and win.

Laila doesn't plan to take that kind of beating.

"My dad was the greatest, but boxing has evolved so much," Laila said. "He fought before a lot of the fighters had the excellent defensive skills they have now. He could get away with things you're now taught not to do."

Besides, a couple of shots to the nose wouldn't be bad. "I have a cute nose already," Laila said playfully. "If it's moved a little to the left or a little to the right, it will still be cute."

For several months, Laila concentrated on training—running, shadowboxing, working the punching bags. She cut back on her social life and dedicated herself to preparing for her first fight. She did take a break, however, to attend her father's 57th birthday party.

At the party she noticed a man stealing glances at her. Johnny "Ya Ya" McClain, a retired cruiserweight boxing champion was attracted to Laila from the first glance. She was tall, beautiful, funny, and shared his passion for boxing. Laila did not return his admiration—at least at first.

"The vibe she was giving me, any normal guy would have been like, 'Forget this girl,'" Ya Ya said later.

Ya Ya told his mother he liked Laila.

His mother then told Muhammad, "I think my son likes your daughter."

"I don't blame him!" Muhammad replied.

Ya Ya asked Laila out. Surprisingly, she said yes. They went to a restaurant together, and Ya Ya nearly blew his chances.

"When the waitress asked how I like my coffee, I said, 'I like my coffee like my women . . . light and sweet.' Laila thought I was an obnoxious jerk."

Laila overlooked Ya Ya's unfortunate comment and the two began dating. Soon Ya Ya agreed to help train Laila and be her assistant manager. They worked in the gym every day together.

"Laila boxes so well," Ya Ya said. "She moves fluently in the ring. She's got long arms and a great jab. She's definitely a natural."

Everyday, Laila ran two miles, then worked out at the gym for two hours. She cut out fried foods and a social life and dedicated herself to learning boxing skills and hardening her body at the L.A. Boxing Gym.

As her first fight approached, Laila stepped up her training and traveled to her father's private gym on his 81-acre spread in Michigan. Laila was eager to show her father what she was learning. At 5 feet 10 inches, Laila had honed her 170-pound body into fighting shape.

Muhammad dropped by to spar with his daughter now and then, giving her pointers.

Laila kept those pointers a secret. "I don't ever tell anybody what those tips are," she said. "When 'The Greatest' tells you something in private, you don't share it with nobody."

As the date of Laila's first fight approached, the press became more and more interested. Some boxing observers said Laila was just what the struggling sport needed.

Laila "will be a huge shot in the arm for women's boxing," said Shelley Williams, commissioner of the International Female Boxers Association. "She has the looks, and I think she can fight, which is not a combination you see too often."

But others were pessimistic. They assumed Laila had more pedigree than fighting skills. They said she would hurt the sport by drawing attention away from proven fighters. Her good looks also worked against her at times. Some people assumed a beautiful woman couldn't be a good fighter.

"A lot of people say that I'm just Muhammad Ali's daughter, and I can't fight," Laila said. "But I know I can fight."

"Right now, people don't know me. They say, 'We'll see what she can do.' Well, I can't wait to get in the ring and show them."

And Laila did show them. That night when she ducked under the ropes to knock out April in the first round, Laila proved she was more than a pretty face and a famous name. Some people saw her father's quick thinking and aggression. Even before the fight, the nickname "Madame Butterfly" was pinned on Laila. It drew on her father's famous "float like a butterfly, sting like a bee" slogan. At a press conference just before her first fight, Laila said she did not like the nickname. The name, however, stuck.

But despite her first win, Laila had a long way to go. April was an easy opponent, picked to give Laila an easy win. Choosing less than challenging competition is common for up-and-coming fighters. Laila still had to prove she could handle a competent opponent.

Laila's second fight was nearly as easy as her first. Laila went up against Shadina Pennybaker, an accounting student from Pittsburgh. They fought at the Mountaineer Race Track and Gaming Resort in Chester, West Virginia, on November 10, 1999.

Again Laila wore a white, hooded robe with "Ali" stitched across the back. She sashayed around the ring, shuffling her boxing shoes. Her white trunks with black piping were also emblazoned with "Ali" on the back just like her father's had been. A little wreath of tattooed flowers encircled her wrist.

Shadina, four inches shorter than Laila, reached out for the first punch. Laila just smiled and shook her head.

Like her father had, Laila verbally sparred with her opponent during the match. After one of Shadina's punches connected, Laila taunted her by saying the punch hadn't been strong enough to feel.

It was a four-round match, and Laila needed nearly four rounds to knock Shadina out. She did it with just three seconds left in the last round. The referee stopped the match after

Laila's flurry of combinations knocked Shadina's mouth protection piece to the canvas floor and blood spattered from her lips. Laila won by technical knockout. A technical knock-out occurs when a referee, fighter, or trainer stops the fight because one fighter is obviously losing. It's a way to keep boxers from needless-ly taking punches.

Laila had a little "mouse"(cut) under her right eye.

After the fight, about twenty reporters and photographers crowded around Laila for a press conference while about thirty fans lined up for autographs. Meanwhile, Laila's entourage sold "She Bee Stinging" T-shirts for $15.

While Laila trained, she and Ya Ya grew clos-er. Ya Ya, who is 10 years older than Laila, said that she was just the woman he needed. She could have the most expensive car made, but drives a Ford pickup truck. She could party with Hollywood's in-crowd, but prefers to spend time playing with her three dogs—a Rottweiler and two Shepherds.

"She's the most down-to-earth woman I've ever met," Ya Ya said. "She keeps it real."

One November evening while they were hav-ing dinner at a Beverly Hills restaurant, Ya Ya got down on his knees and asked Laila to be his wife. She said yes. A couple sitting nearby over-heard and sent over two glasses of champagne.

Ya Ya drank both glasses, knowing a fighter in training shouldn't be drinking, and the cou-ple began to plan their wedding. They set a date for August and buckled down for the next fight.

Laila dominated her third fight as well. On December 10, she faced Nicolyn Armstrong in

Detroit. It was Nicolyn's first professional fight, but she out-weighed Laila by 13 pounds.

Laila knocked Nicolyn down in the first round with a left jab and three hard rights, but Nicolyn got back up. In the second round, Laila landed a left-right combination to give her another technical knockout win.

Laila raised her arms in victory, knowing that after three straight knock-out wins, she was on her way.

# 5

# BAD INTENTIONS

Three months later, on March 7, 2000, Laila was back near Detroit, at the Casino Windsor in Ontario, facing Crystal Arcand. Crystal had won all five of her amateur matches.

The night before the fight, Laila trained at a local gym in her usual way. She'd already done the sit-ups, the heavy bag pounding, and the speed bag. Now she was jumping rope.

"Pick it up, pick it up. Let's go, baby. Faster," her trainer barked.

Laila's long braids bounced with each jump. Hip-hop music played in the background. Her gray track pants were stained with sweat. Laila missed, tangling her feet in the rope. She shook her head and smiled.

When she left the gym, regulars came with boxing gloves they wanted her to sign. Laila cheerfully spent a few minutes scrawling her name on the leather.

But during her fights, Laila was a lot more careful about giving her name and image away. Laila and her management team barred any videocameras at her fights, as they

Not all Laila's wins have come by knockout. Her bout against Kendra Lenhart of Tennessee went the distance, but Laila continued her unbeaten streak, winning by unanimous decision.

had at previous fights. Only her own camera crew filmed her matches, preparing a video for sale. Laila's camp intended to build suspense and make as much money from Laila's fans as possible.

"There's going to be no TV, not while I'm still learning," Laila told a reporter before the fight. "Got to get up there, then it will be the big deal. It's all very much planned. It has to be."

"Nobody is going to exploit me. Nobody can do that to me, or the people around me."

Laila knew her father had been used by those around him to make money and achieve fame. She also knew that fame had taken its toll on Muhammad.

Being close to fame all her life made Laila wary of the limelight. She didn't want to forfeit her privacy to fame, but knew there would be a trade-off.

"Of course I wanna make my name—that's why I go to the gym every day," Laila said. "But I never ever wanted to be famous, because my dad is the most famous man in the world, and I see how he has no privacy."

At the same time, Laila understood that fame was taking her places and giving her attention she'd never have enjoyed without her name.

"Well, my name is always gonna open doors," Laila said. "I can't help that, and of course I'm gonna walk through them. I'm not gonna say, 'Oh no, I'm trying to prove a point.' Of course I'm gonna get paid more, of course I'm gonna get more attention, but a lot of responsibility comes with that. Not everybody could handle what I go through—being in the public eye, speaking at fundraisers for kids— not everyone has the personality."

Muhammad has tried to help his daughter deal with the fame. "The main thing my dad

Laila works on her moves, shadowboxing in the gym as her trainer Dub Huntly and boyfriend Johnny "Ya Ya" McClain look on.

gives me is life advice, just how to deal with people, how to deal with being in the public eye, not letting it go to your head," Laila said.

Keeping the attention and fame within bounds was important to Laila. From the beginning of her career, she worked to control her own image. This match would be no different.

Laila waited for the match to begin while the now-familiar feelings came.

"Before a fight, there's so much tension and anticipation, I think, 'Why do I put myself through this?'" Laila said. "Then during the fight, you find that you love it. And you can't wait for more."

To "psyche" herself, Laila listened to hard-core rap music and thought mean thoughts.

"I have bad intentions when I'm in the ring," she said. "You do have to be an angry person. I think all the bad, angry thoughts I can. I don't know where it comes from. It just happens."

When the opening bell rang, Laila circled Crystal and landed a combination ending in an uppercut that sent Crystal to the canvas after only 15 seconds. Crystal rose quickly and came back at Laila. Laila landed a straight right to the top of Crystal's head that dropped her one minute into the round. Although she struggled to one knee, Crystal couldn't beat the count.

Laila needed only 64 seconds to knock out Crystal. Laila reportedly received $25,000 for the fight, while Crystal received only $5,000. Laila's name, and the fans that it drew, were worth more.

"I underestimated her," Crystal said later. "She's got the power and she can back it up. I've never experienced a woman with the amount of power she has."

Laila was disappointed the match ended so quickly.

"I wanted to jab more," she said. "Work a little more in the ring. I wanted to work on controlling the person. I wanted to work on my feet and taking my time."

After the fight, Laila wrapped some of her father's famous bravado around herself for the press conference. "I'm stronger than my dad was, comparably as a woman," Laila said. "People just aren't used to it and can't take it."

"No matter who you put in the ring, I'm going to knock them out!"

Between fights, Laila trained hard. Six days a week she woke up at 6 A.M. and headed out for a four-mile run. Afterwards, she went to the gym for a three-hour workout. She sweated through 500 sit-ups, shadowboxed, and then hit the heavy bag and the speed bag. She topped off each workout with four to eight rounds of sparring. She often sparred with men because most of the women at her gym were too small for her.

To keep her body fat low, she ate mostly salads and low-fat meats like turkey and chicken. Laila missed apple pie and vanilla ice cream most of all but knew that lean muscle mass was crucial in the ring.

Laila also knew that many of the skills she needed were mental. She needed to keep her head while taking punches, whether the crowd booed or cheered or was silent.

"I run and I work out in the gym every day," Laila said. "This sport takes determination and confidence, and you have to have that fighting instinct. I can't explain what this is, but I have it."

"If things don't go your way, you gotta be able to deal with it, you gotta be able to keep going, you gotta be able to tune out the crowd," Laila said. "A lot of the time people get hyped up by the crowd and start trying to play into it and don't do what's smart in the ring."

Laila tuned out the crowd and heard only Ya Ya's voice when she was in the ring. She saw only Ya Ya and her opponent. When she spoke in the ring, it was for her opponent only, never to the crowd.

In April, Laila was back in Detroit. By now she was traveling with an entourage of people— her doctor, trainer and assistant, press agent, valet, photographer, bodyguard, and sparring partner. She preferred to travel by white limousine. Ya Ya was always by her side. He quickly gained a reputation of being affectionate and protective with Laila but sometimes belligerent with others.

It was Laila's fifth fight and the first time that she faced a worthy opponent. When Laila entered the ring with Karen Bill, a 166-pound fighter from Oklahoma City who had fought five times before, Laila had her first real challenge.

Rain soaked the Joe Louis Arena in Detroit that night. Eight thousand boxing fans were already a bit bored after the first fight of the night, a tedious men's light heavyweight match. Laila entered the room from a door leading from the dressing room. A floor-length, hooded white robe draped her tall frame. She walked down the aisle toward the ring, flanked by trainers and bodyguards. Heads turned, pulses quickened.

At the ring, Laila shrugged off her robe, displaying her 5-foot-10, 168-pound body, clad in a white sports bra and white satin shorts. Fans watched her broad shoulders and firm muscles as she climbed into the ring. Her hair braided into cornrows, she was ready to fight.

Laila glanced down at her father in a ringside seat. Five minutes before the fight, Muhammad had entered the arena as the crowd chanted his name. He hadn't seen her fight since her debut. He caught Laila's eyes as she shadowboxed to warm up.

The bell rang, beginning the four-round fight. Karen had several disadvantages. She was 10 years older than Laila and two inches shorter. But she was strong, with the powerful arms of a former nationally ranked hammer thrower. She moved forward to attack.

Laila and Karen exchanged a barrage of punches to the head and face. Laila tried to circle, jabbing away, but the fight looked more like a brawl than boxing.

Halfway into round two, Karen threw a right uppercut that caught Laila. She fell to the mat, stunned.

The crowd began to chant, "Al-Ali! Al-Ali! Al-Ali!" Laila jumped up, refusing to stay down for the full eight seconds a fighter can take and still remain in the fight. She knew that staying down would have given her a chance to rest, but the urge to fight was too strong.

The third round was Laila's. Her blows to Karen's face came fast and furious. The crowd roared as the women charged and punched.

Laila's nose bled slightly, but Karen's face was covered with blood. The referee stepped in to stop the fight near the end of the third, two-minute round.

He raised Laila's glove in triumph, giving her a third-round technical knockout over Karen.

Laila jumped from the ring to hug her father as the crowd chanted "Ali! Ali! Ali!"

"I think he called me a warrior, but I'm not really sure," Laila said afterwards.

Karen left the ring disappointed. The referee shouldn't have stopped the fight, she said later.

"I wasn't surprised that they stopped it, because of who she is," Karen said. "But I was really upset. I was winning the fight, and I was still throwing punches. Yes, I was getting hit, but this is boxing. You're going to get hit. That's the point."

Laila, however, was glad the referee intervened.

"Some people think they should never stop a fight," she said. "Those are the people that get all beat up and punchy."

The next morning Laila talked about the fight with a reporter at her hotel.

"That was by far my toughest fight," she said.

"She caught me off guard. But my legs were fine. I just hopped up.

"I never, ever pictured myself getting knocked down. All I could think was, 'I've got to get her.'"

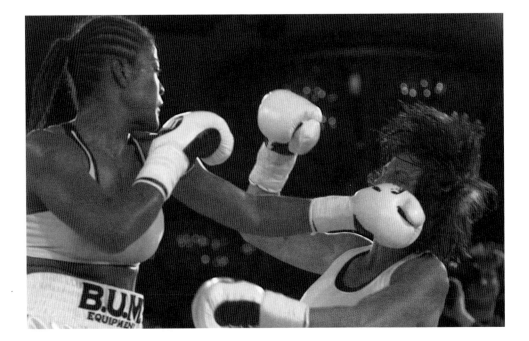

# 6

# DRAWING CROWDS

Laila's sixth fight would take place halfway around the world in China. The Chinese are not boxing fans as a group. Many of them think boxing is a blood sport that degrades the people who watch—especially people who watch women fight.

Nevertheless the stadium in the southern city of Guangzhou was at least half full when Laila arrived in April to show her stuff. Several men's fights were on the card that night. Boxing cards are the list of matches planned for a particular night of fighting. Laila's match would be the only women's fight, and the crowd seemed more interested in Laila than in the other fighters.

Before the fight a reporter asked Laila if she hoped to inspire Chinese women to be more aggressive and athletic.

"Honestly, it's not that I hope to do that," Laila answered. "I just want to be the best that I can be. I'm not setting out to be this big conqueror of women's boxing. A fight is a fight. It doesn't really matter to me where it is taking place. No matter where it is set up, I just show up."

Since her well-publicized bout against Jacqui Frazier-Lyde, Laila has continued her winning ways. Here, she knocks out challenger Christine Robinson in the fourth round.

Laila faced Kristina King, an American police SWAT-team member and former prison guard from Michigan. Laila dominated the match. Kristina's face was bloody and swollen after Laila's repeated blows. The referee stopped the fight near the beginning of the fourth and final round, giving Laila another technical knockout victory. The fight also gave Laila her first television appearance, on the Showtime cable channel.

Laila raised her arms in victory and relayed a message to her father through the press. "I did it for you, Dad," she said.

On June 15, Laila fought for the first time in her hometown of Los Angeles. Her fight against Marjorie Jones of Milwaukee shared the card with several men's matches, including five-time world champion Oscar de la Hoya's bout.

Sitting ringside was Muhammad, along with two of his former opponents, Joe Frazier and Ken Norton. The 3,500 fans at the Universal Amphitheater began chanting his name and rose to a standing ovation when they spotted Muhammad. His wife, Lonnie, and at least three of his daughters sat beside him. Laila's mother, Veronica was also sitting near the ring.

Laila's fight was over before she even warmed up. The bell rang. Laila circled to the left. Marjorie missed a punch. Laila threw a right and Marjorie went down. Laila threw another right and Marjorie went down a second time in the first minute. Sixty-eight seconds into the first round, Laila connected with a right to Marjorie's head. The 48-year-old fell and the referee didn't even bother to count her out. It was over.

Another boxing dynasty—former heavy-weight champ Joe Frazier with his boxing daughter Jacqui Frazier-Lyde.

"I feel good, but of course I would have liked it to last longer," Laila said. "I told the referee to let me knock her out."

With her seventh win, Laila was now ranked fifth among all women middleweights. She could afford a brief break for her personal life.

In August Laila was training for a very different kind of event—her wedding.

Her sister, Hana, led the wedding procession on August 27. Laila's nephew and Ya Ya's nephew followed carrying grass pillows topped with rings. Ya Ya's 10-year-old daughter from his first marriage and his six-year-old niece followed, dropping rose petals along the aisle.

Laila, dressed in a white, crystal-beaded sheath dress, took her father's arm. They walked down the petal-strewn aisle, flanked by 275 guests. Laila lifted her veil and kissed Muhammad's cheek as they reached the front.

"Who is it who gives this woman to this man?" the minister asked. Muhammad raised his right hand.

The minister handed Laila and Ya Ya each a white rose. He told the couple to place the flower, a symbol of "love and purity of intention" in a special place at home as a reminder "that love has the final word."

Laila's eyes teared as he spoke. But later Laila quipped, "We're going to need a lot of those roses."

At the reception in the Pasadena Ritz-Carlton Hotel's ballroom, many of boxing's royalty danced to celebrate the union. Tiny white leather boxing gloves were given out as wedding favors.

Laila and Ya Ya found a two-bedroom townhouse in L.A. and began married life together. They had to put off their honeymoon, however, to prepare for the next fight.

On October 20, Laila faced Kendra Lenhart in Auburn Hills, Michigan. They were fighting on the undercard of Mike Tyson and Andrew Golota and were broadcast on Showtime.

With her father watching ringside, Laila stepped into the ring. Kendra was a worthy opponent. The two were informed just before the fight that they would be fighting six rounds instead of the traditional four because of Michigan law. Laila and Kendra traded fierce punches during the first three rounds. By the sixth round, both had taken blows and were tiring.

When the fight ended, judges tallied their scores and Laila came out the winner by unanimous decision. When one fighter doesn't knock another down for the count of eight, ring judges tally the number of punches each fighter landed. The boxer with the most points is declared the winner. If all judges agree, the decision is called unanimous. It was the first time Laila hadn't won by knockout.

By now Laila was more than a famous name. She had won eight professional fights—a few of them against tough competitors.

Many of her detractors realized she was more than a famous name and a pretty face. Some people were saying that Laila would create an explosion of interest in women's boxing and turn it into a thriving sport.

Laila disagreed. While her name can help, Laila said, what the sport needs is a lot of good boxers.

"I think what it's going to take is for women, as individuals to learn how to box," Laila said. "Learn how to really develop their boxing skills. . . . I can bring more people to watch women's boxing who normally would not watch it. That could be a start, but it's not going to be just me."

Besides, Laila said, women's boxing will never be as popular as men's because so many people don't think women should be taking punches.

"I'm not gonna be the one to change their minds, you know what I'm saying?" Laila said. "Some people are never gonna get used to the idea—men who don't like seeing powerful women. And women who think it's unladylike. If you don't like it, basically what it comes down to is you don't watch it."

"The same thing all female sports suffer from: [people say] women shouldn't be doing this. If you are doing it, then maybe you are too masculine or you are gay. They cannot take boxing just for what it is: that you want to box, that this is what you like to do. I'm not paying much attention to it because I'm not one of those women who ever had a problem within myself. That's why I don't feel this pressure: 'Oh, we need to do this for women's boxing. I just think, 'I want to box,' and I box, you know?"

Along with more skilled women boxers, the sport needs money to lure qualified competitors. Women usually make a fraction of what men make. While top fighters like Christy Martin earn $100,000 to $150,000 a match, most make only $300 a round.

Laila falls somewhere in between. She's made between $10,000 and $25,000 for most of her fights. And the money, Laila has always admitted, is part of the attraction. She plans to fight for five years, make as much as she can, and retire.

"I'm not doing it just for the money," she says, "but I want what I'm worth. I'm not going to have promoters making money off me and not get any of it myself."

The biggest checks for many athletes don't come from their professional sports but from becoming spokespeople for products. Laila managed to grab two advertising promotion jobs. B.U.M. Equipment and Dr. Pepper both hired her to promote their products. They hope that Laila's looks and tough-girl career will appeal to young urban buyers.

She's also had offers to model and appear in television and film. But for the next few years Laila plans to continue building confidence and skills. She'll eventually have to fight proven boxers like Diane Clark, Valerie Mahfood and Kathy Rivers. Then the real test of Laila's skills and pedigree will begin.

Once she wins the title, Laila plans to defend it a few times and then stop. She wants to retire to raising children and running a business that creates jobs in inner-city Los Angeles.

*7*

# HER EYES; HIS EYES

Laila's decision to box has sparked a trend in women's boxing. Since her debut, three more daughters of famed boxers have turned pro. Actually, Laila wasn't first—only the most famous. J'Marie Moore, daughter of former light-heavyweight champ Archie Moore, debuted two years before Laila.

Laila expected the trend. "I knew other women were gonna start fighting when I started fighting," she said. "Not only 'cause they wanna fight, because a lot of 'em wanna fight me."

Shortly after Laila's third fight, Jacqui Frazier-Lyde, the daughter of heavyweight Joe Frazier, announced she was entering boxing. Freeda Foreman, the daughter of heavyweight champion George Foreman, has also jumped in the ring. The third famous daughter to follow Laila was Irichelle Duran, lightweight champion Roberto Duran's daughter.

But Laila will have to contend with only one of these fighters. Jacqui is the only fighter close to Laila's weight

Laila's bout against Frazier-Lyde was by no means an easy one for Ali. Here she gets tagged as she attempts to dodge a punch. But when it was all over, the judges awarded the decision to Laila.

class. For boxing fans, the prospect of these two women fighting is special.

The urge to carry on the Frazier-Ali grudge had survived decades. Joe Frazier and Muhammad Ali fought three times in the 1970s, with Joe winning one match and Muhammad winning two. Their third and most famous fight, known as "The Thrilla in Manila," is legendary. Muhammad won when Joe didn't come out of the corner for the 15th round. Their fights are considered among the most interesting in boxing history.

When Jacqui went pro, the potential match between the famous heavyweights' daughters caught the boxing world's attention. Jacqui capitalized on the grudge from the beginning.

"It's about history, competition, family and legacy," Jacqui said when asked about fighting Laila. "I love it. But don't get me wrong. I'm gonna love watching her go down. I'm going to kick Laila's butt. That's what Fraziers do. We kick Ali butt."

Laila, however, didn't take the bait. She considered Jacqui beneath her.

Jacqui is a lawyer in her late 30s with three children. She is 17 years older than Laila and nearly 20 pounds heavier. Even after Jacqui won her first three fights easily, Laila didn't take her seriously. Even if Jacqui came down in weight, she would not be much of a challenge, Laila said.

"I would just beat her around and then what?" Laila said. "She knows people will pay to see us fight. But after that, she's done, and I will move on from that to fight more. I want to be the champion of my weight class and in order to improve, you have to fight people who challenge you."

But that won't be easy. In Laila's weight division, 160 to 168 pounds, opponents are limited. Most of the experienced female fighters—Christy Martin, Lucia Rijker, Kathy Collins and Jane Couch—are welterweights, who weigh 30 pounds less than Laila.

After taking Jacqui's taunts in the press for several months, Laila agreed to take her on. After all there would be lots of attention and money for such a high profile fight.

"[Jacqui]'s like a little fly that just won't go away," Ya Ya explained. "You have her constantly bothering you and calling you names. It's only fitting that Laila would take this challenge and get rid of her."

Laila and Jacqui held a joint press conference in February 2001 to announce their intention to fight in June 2001.

At first, Jacqui seemed to try to make the occasion friendly. She brought out a heart-shaped cake and made an endearing speech about her rival that put a smile on Laila's face. But as Jacqui—who had now won all six of her pro fights—neared the end of her speech she suddenly slammed her fist into the middle of the cake, grinning. "I'm going to eat that body up," she said. "She's not going to be able to walk the same."

Laila appeared unfazed by Jacqui's showmanship, which included several bicep flexes. Laila ignored Jacqui throughout the hour-long conference.

"I knew she was going to try to do something because she had to do something to try to get attention," Laila said. "What's it going to take to put her down? Not much. I'm actually going to try to drag it out to the end so I can whup her, put a beating on her."

Raising her hands in victory, Laila celebrates her win by majority decision over Jacqui Frazier-Lyde. Three decades earlier, Ali's father fought Frazier's (heavyweight champ Joe Frazier) for the first time.

Laila calls the trend of famed daughters entering boxing "annoying." And many agree with her. Some critics say that Laila and other boxing daughters denigrate the new sport into a spectacle. It's the famous-name crowd that gets the attention while proven fighters like Christy Martin and Lucia Rijker go unnoticed.

"It's women capitalizing on their father's names, on their sexuality and not going out there and doing what some of the other women have done," said Stan Hoffman, Rijker's manager.

"These are women who spent years and years learning their trade like the guys do. These women paid their dues and can seriously fight."

Laila counters that she is paying her dues and she has proven she can fight. The fact that she's attractive shouldn't make her efforts seem frivolous.

"It really has nothing to do with looks," she said. "Do I have to look ugly because I want to box? Would they [dare] say that to my opponent? I don't think it's fair to say this—and it hurts me! Sometimes I feel bad because people always make me [out] to be the pretty one, and that really has nothing to do with fighting. A fight is a fight. It doesn't matter what you look like."

Part of what made Muhammad so famous, however, was his good looks and his popularity.

"Boxing, male or female, has always depended on stars," argues veteran boxing journalist Katherine Dunn. "If Laila Ali can perform, she'll be a great asset to the sport, both as a role model and as a media magnet."

On March 2, Laila and Jacqui were together again in the same ring. Both were fighting other opponents on the same card at the Turning Stone Casino in New York.

Laila faced Christine Robinson, a tough competitor. In the first four rounds, both fighters traded blows. By the fifth round, Laila landed a series of brutal punches while the crowd chanted "Ali! Ali! Ali!" Christine went down and Laila won her ninth fight by a knockout.

Jacqui also won her fight by a knockout in the first round, giving her seven wins all by knockout.

After their fights, the women held a news conference to promote their match in June 2001. They kept up their verbal slug-fest.

"It only took me one round to finish my opponent," Jacqui said.

"As you all saw," Laila answered, "our opponents were on two totally different levels. So that tells me nothing."

"I hope her coach teaches her how to take a punch," Jacqui said.

"Girlfriend," Laila barked, "you ain't got nothing for me, OK?"

**** 

Laila, wrapped in a canary-yellow scarf, was waiting in the casino lounge before a fight when Ted Tehensky, a businessman in his 60s, noticed her. He stared and stared before tentatively asking if he could shake her hand. She turned a radiant smile on him and he began to cry.

"I just think it's great what you're doing," said the man who had once boxed as an amateur and watched all of Muhammad's fights. "Keep on winning."

"Oh, I will," Laila said. "Now don't go getting too emotional."

Mr. Tehensky was shocked by his tears. "I couldn't control it, and I'm a hardened businessman," he said later. "Looking in her eyes—her eyes and his eyes, they're a matching pair. Who would ever have dreamed, that his daughter would be fighting, of all things."

A reporter asked Laila if this sort of encounter happened often.

"All the time," she said quietly.

# STATISTICS

| Date | Place | Winner | kind of win | round |
|------|-------|--------|-------------|-------|
| 10/08/99 | Verona, NY | Laila Ali | KO | 1 |
| 11/10/99 | Chester, WV | Laila Ali | TKO | 4 |
| 12/10/99 | Detroit, MI | Laila Ali | TKO | 2 |
| 03/07/00 | Windsor, Canada | Laila Ali | KO | 1 |
| 04/08/00 | Detroit, MI | Laila Ali | TKO | 3 |
| 04/22/00 | Guangzhou, China | Laila Ali | TKO | 4 |
| 06/15/00 | Los Angeles, CA | Laila Ali | TKO | 3 |
| 10/20/00 | Detroit, MI | Laila Ali | UD | 6 |
| 3/02/01 | New York | Laila Ali | KO | 5 |

# CHRONOLOGY

| | |
|---|---|
| Dec. 30, 1977 | Laila Ali is born in Los Angeles. |
| 1986 | Parents divorce; Laila lives with her mother. |
| 1996 | Sees her first women's boxing match. |
| 1999 | Announces intention to be a professional boxer. |
| Nov. 10, 1999 | Wins first match with a knockout. |
| Dec. 10, 1999 | Wins second match with a technical knockout. |
| March 7, 2000 | Wins fourth match with a knockout. |
| April 8, 2000 | Knocked to the mat for the first time, but wins by technical knockout. |
| April 22, 2000 | Fights in China, winning by technical knockout. |
| June 15, 2000 | Fights in hometown of Los Angeles and wins by knockout. |
| Aug. 27, 2000 | Marries assistant trainer and manager, Johnny "Ya Ya" McClain. |
| Oct. 20, 2000 | Wins eighth fight by unanimous decision. |
| March 2, 2001 | Wins ninth fight by knockout; announces intention to fight Jacqui Frazier. |

# FURTHER READING

Ali, Hana. *More Than a Hero: Muhammad Ali's Life Lessons Presented Through His Daughter's Eyes.* New York: Pocket Books, 2000.

Ali, Muhammad and Richard Durham. *The Greatest: My Own Story.* New York: Random House, 1975.

Bacho, Peter. *Boxing in Black and White.* New York: Henry Holt, 1999.

Sekules, Kate. *The Boxer's Heart: How I fell in Love with the Ring.* Village Books, 2000.

Tessitore, John. *Muhammad Ali: The World's Champion.* Library Binding, 1998.

# INDEX

# ABOUT THE AUTHOR

CINDY DYSON has written several biographies for young adults. She lives in Montana with her husband and son.

HANNAH STORM, NBC Sports play-by-play announcer, reporter, and studio host, made her debut in 1992 at Wimbledon during the All England Tennis Championships. Shortly thereafter, she was paired with Jim Lampley to cohost the *Olympic Show* for the 1992 Olympic Games in Barcelona. Later that year, Storm was named cohost of *Notre Dame Saturday*, NBC's college football pregame show. Adding to her repertoire, Storm became a reporter for the 1994 Major League All-Star Game and the pregame host for the 1995, 1997, and 1999 World Series. Storm's success as host of *NBA Showtime* during the 1997–98 season won her the role as studio host for the inaugural season of the Women's National Basketball Association in 1998.

In 1996, Storm was selected as NBC's host for the Summer Olympics in Atlanta, and she has been named as host for both the 2000 Summer Olympics in Sydney and the 2002 Winter Olympics in Salt Lake City. Storm received a Gracie Allen Award for Outstanding Personal Achievement, which was presented by the American Women in Radio and Television Foundation (AWRTF), for her coverage of the 1999 NBA Finals and 1999 World Series. She has been married to NBC Sports broadcaster Dan Hicks since 1994. They have two daughters.